WOMEN

NO

WE MARCH FOR JOBS FOR ALL NOW!

EDS

RDS

THE CULPEPER MINUTE MEN

LIBERTY

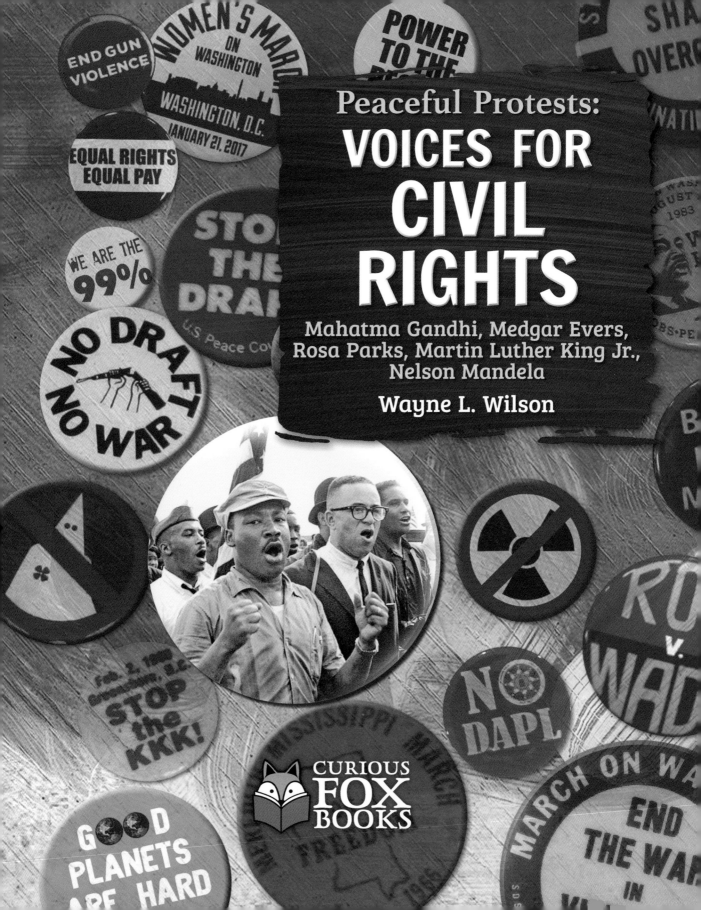

Peaceful Protests:

VOICES FOR CIVIL RIGHTS

Mahatma Gandhi, Medgar Evers,
Rosa Parks, Martin Luther King Jr.,
Nelson Mandela

Wayne L. Wilson

CURIOUS FOX BOOKS

ABOUT THE AUTHOR

Wayne L. Wilson has written numerous biographical and historical books for children and young adults. He received a Master of Arts in education with a specialization in sociology and anthropology from UCLA. He is also a screenwriter and member of the Writer's Guild of America.

© 2024 by Curious Fox Books™, an imprint of Fox Chapel Publishing Company, Inc., 903 Square Street, Mount Joy, PA 17552.

Peaceful Protests: Voices for Civil Rights is a revision of *I Protest: A History of Peaceful Protest: Voices for Civil Rights*, published in 2018 by Purple Toad Publishing, Inc. Reproduction of its contents is strictly prohibited without written permission from the rights holder.

Paperback ISBN 979-8-89094-018-6
Hardcover ISBN 979-8-89094-019-3

Library of Congress Control Number: 2023947035

To learn more about the other great books from Fox Chapel Publishing, or to find a retailer near you, call toll-free 800-457-9112 or visit us at *www.FoxChapelPublishing.com*.

We are always looking for talented authors. To submit an idea, please send a brief inquiry to acquisitions@foxchapelpublishing.com.

Fox Chapel Publishing makes every effort to use environmentally friendly paper for printing.

Printed in Malaysia

CONTENTS

CHAPTER ONE
Civil Rights Protests—
The Beginnings

If there is no struggle, there is no progress.
—Frederick Douglass[1]

The history of the African American civil rights movement features brave individuals and groups of people. At times the battles against racism and prejudice have led to violence; but many famous victories for equal rights were the result of passive resistance.

In the early 1800s in the United States, black and white abolitionists publicly protested against slavery and racial injustice. They wrote and distributed pamphlets and newspapers demanding an end to slavery. Women walked door to door in many Northern neighborhoods, asking people to sign their antislavery petitions.

The Birth of a Nation Protest

In 1909, a new civil rights organization was formed. It was called the National Association for the Advancement of Colored People (NAACP). The organization's purpose was to fight against racial discrimination and to provide equal rights for all people.

On April 11, 1851, abolitionist Wendell Phillips protested the case of fugitive slave Thomas Sims, attempting to keep him from being returned to slavery. His effort failed, but it was still an important early attempt at protecting the human rights.

Its black and white founders included W.E.B. Du Bois, Mary White Ovington, Ida B. Wells-Barnett, and Dr. Henry Moskowitz.[2]

One of the NAACP's early national campaigns was against D.W. Griffith's technologically groundbreaking but problematic film *The Birth of a Nation*. Based on the 1905 book *The Clansman*, this racist film glorified the Ku Klux Klan. African Americans were shown in the film as rapists, dumb politicians, and stupidly loyal servants. Black characters were played by white people in blackface. President Woodrow Wilson, a segregationist, highly praised the film when it premiered in early 1915. The NAACP wanted the film to be censored.[3]

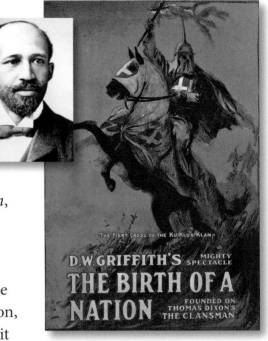

W.E.B. Du Bois (left) and a poster for *The Birth of a Nation*.

In 1915, William Monroe Trotter, civil rights leader and editor of *The Guardian* newspaper, opposed the film when it showed in Boston. Trotter and the NAACP staged 18 mass rallies ranging from 500 to 2,500 protesters each. They demonstrated in front of Boston's Faneuil Hall, rallied on the Boston Common, marched on the State House, and held picket signs in front of Boston's Tremont Theatre.[4]

Even though the film was considered a success, some cities refused to show it because of the demonstrations. Activists realized there was power in mass protests. Membership in the NAACP continued to grow.

The East St. Louis Riot Protest

In East St. Louis, Illinois, on July 1, 1917, violence broke out after failed labor strikes. When white workers went on strike to protest labor conditions, the company hired black workers to replace them. Furious, white mobs burned buildings and attacked black men, women, and children. Up to 200 people were likely killed and hundreds injured during this bloody riot. Thousands of black citizens fled from their homes in fear and at least 6,000 African American residents were left homeless. Hundreds of thousands of dollars' worth of damage was done to homes and buildings in African American communities in East St. Louis.

In response, the NAACP conducted its first major civil rights protest. Led by lawyer James Weldon Johnson, 10,000 black men, women, and children marched down Fifth Avenue in New York City in a "Silent Protest Parade."[5]

The New York Times described the Saturday march as "one of the most orderly demonstrations ever witnessed." About 20,000 blacks and some whites lined the route. They watched in silence as people marched 36 blocks from Fifty-Ninth Street and Fifth Avenue to Madison Square Park near the Flatiron Building. The only sound was the slow muffled beating of drums.[6]

The NAACP organized a Silent Parade on July 28, 1917, in response to the East St. Louis riots. Ten thousand African Americans participated in this protest march.

Eight hundred children dressed in white led the parade. Next came women, also dressed in white. The men dressed in black. Their banners and signs read: "Mother, do lynchers go to heaven?"; "Give me a chance to live"; "Color, blood, and suffering have made us one"; and "America has lynched without trial 2,867 Negroes in 31 years and not a single murderer has suffered."

The Jack Spratt Coffee House Sit-In

The first organized civil rights "sit-in" in American history happened in May 1943. A local diner in Chicago, Jack Spratt, would not serve black customers. James Farmer studied Indian nationalist leader Mohandas Gandhi's strategy of nonviolent action. He decided to test this approach on the diner. He, George Houser, and Bernice Fisher formed a group named the Congress of Racial Equality (CORE). They would protest with a sit-in.

Twenty-eight people entered Jack Spratt in groups of two, three, and four. In each party there was at least one black man or woman.[7] In these groups, no whites ate until the black people were served. In some groups, the whites would hand their plate to the black person nearest them. The manager offered to serve all the "colored" people in the basement if they would go there, but the customers politely refused. He offered to serve them if they would move to the back corner of the diner. He was again declined. The frustrated manager phoned the police. The police refused to kick the group out and left. Finally, the CORE members were served the food they ordered.

CORE went back to the restaurant days later and found that Jack Spratt's

James Farmer in 1965. His actions earned him the Presidential Medal of Freedom in 1998.

policy of not serving African Americans had changed. It was a small but important victory.

The Journey of Reconciliation

In 1946, the Supreme Court declared that segregation in interstate travel was unconstitutional. But this ruling was largely ignored in the South. In 1947, CORE and the Fellowship of Reconciliation (FOR) sent eight white and eight black men into the South by bus and train. Activists George Houser and Bayard Rustin organized the two-week "Journey of Reconciliation" through Virginia, North Carolina, Tennessee, and Kentucky.

Bayard Rustin (center, wearing bowtie), George Houser (front, black suit), and other members of the Journey of Reconciliation stand outside the office of Attorney S. W. Robinson. They made the first Freedom Ride in 1947.

Blacks sat in the front and whites in the back, while others sat together, all violations of the states' Jim Crow laws. This resulted in a few separate arrest incidents.[8] In North Carolina, Bayard Rustin and Andrew Johnson were sentenced to 30 days on a chain gang. The judge was harsher with Joe Felmet and Igal Roodenko, two white Jewish activists from New York. The judge said, "Just to teach you a lesson, I gave your black boys thirty days, and I gave you ninety!"[9]

The Journey of Reconciliation received a lot of media attention. In 1948, Houser and Rustin were honored with the Thomas Jefferson Award for the Advancement of Democracy. They received the award because of their efforts to end segregation in interstate travel.

MAHATMA GANDHI

Gandhi, spiritual leader of the Indian independence movement, said: "You must be the change you wish to see in the world."

Mohandas Karamchand Gandhi was born in India in 1869 to an upper-class Hindu family. Known as Mahatma (Great Soul), Gandhi led India to independence from British rule. His belief in passive resistance for change inspired many great civil rights leaders, including Martin Luther King Jr. and Nelson Mandela.

Gandhi's activism began as a young lawyer in South Africa. He was shocked and angered about how horribly Indians were treated by the white British government. In his first court appearance in 1893, he was asked to remove his turban. He refused and walked out of the courtroom. Days later a white man complained about Gandhi sitting in the first-class section of a train and refusing to give up his seat to a white European passenger. Though he had a ticket, he was thrown off the train at the next station. It was then he vowed to fight the "deep disease of color prejudice."[10]

Gandhi studied world religions and Hindu spiritual books. He said, "The religious spirit within me became a living force."[11] He chose to live a simple life. He spun his own clothes with a spinning wheel. He became a vegetarian and devoted time to prayer, fasting, and meditation.

One of the religious principles he learned was *ahimsa* (a-him-sa), which means to "do no harm." Gandhi turned it into a nonviolent tool to resist oppression, calling it *satyagraha* (sat-YAH-graha)—"truth force." Gandhi believed the purpose of using nonviolence as a weapon was to change people's points of view, to win over their minds and hearts.[12]

In South Africa and India, Gandhi organized nonviolent protests against the British Empire. His campaigns involved peaceful demonstrations, sit-ins, picketing, vigils, boycotts, work and hunger strikes, and more.

One of his most successful campaigns was the Salt March. Britain placed a heavy tax on salt, and it hit India's poor people the hardest. On March 12, 1930, Gandhi marched 240 miles to a town by the Arabian Sea called Dandi. Thousands of Indians joined the 24-day march. Gandhi broke the law and made his own salt from seawater. His action inspired similar protests across India. Gandhi and about 60,000 Indians were jailed for breaking the Salt Acts. Mahatma Gandhi became a beloved figure around the world.

Gandhi picks up grains of salt by the sea in the town of Dandi.

CHAPTER TWO
Civil Rights Activities in the 1950s

The Regional Council of Negro Leadership (RCNL) was based in the Mississippi Delta area. It was started in 1951 by Dr. T.R.M. Howard, a very successful African American surgeon and businessman. The Council's mission was to promote programs of civil rights, self-help, and business ownership. It conducted mass meetings with thousands of people.[1]

Civil rights activist Medgar Evers became its program director. In 1952, Evers organized RCNL's first protest—a boycott in the Delta against gas stations that refused to let nonwhites use their restrooms. Protesters issued 20,000 bumper stickers for supporters to put on their cars. Their slogan was, "Don't Buy Gas Where You Can't Use the Restroom."

The organization also protested police brutality and encouraged African American citizens to register to vote.[2]

School Desegregation and Integration
By the early 1950s, many organizations and activists were also working against segregation in public schools. The 1954 Supreme Court decision in Brown v. Board of Education became an

Civil rights activist Medgar Evers was born in 1925 in Mississippi. He worked to overturn segregation at the University of Mississippi Law School and became the first field secretary for the NAACP.

Protesters gather in New York City in October 1955 for the Emmett Till rally. Many people and organizations voiced the need for others to join them and fight against racism and social injustice.

important legal precedent used throughout the fight for civil rights.

Change in education would be long in coming. Later in 1957, the Little Rock Nine were blocked from entering school by order of the Arkansas governor. It would eventually take intervention from President Eisenhower and personal protection from National Guard and Army 101st Airborne soldiers to allow the students to regularly attend their classes.

The Murder of Emmett Till Protest Rally

A horrifying crime committed in the middle of the decade inspired many others to join the fight. In August 1955, while visiting relatives in Mississippi, 14-year-old Emmett Till from Chicago was beaten to death and dumped in a river for allegedly whistling at a white woman. Two white men were arrested for the murder. An all-white jury acquitted them. Later, in 1956, the men bragged about murdering Till in a magazine interview.[3]

Emmett's mother, Mamie Till, wanted justice. She asked that the casket be open at his funeral. She wanted the world to see his horribly bruised and beaten body. Outrage and sympathy poured in from around the world.[4] The shameful verdict led to boycotts and demonstrations.

On October 11, 1955, a massive rally was held in New York City. Led by the NAACP and the District 65 Retail, Wholesale and Department Store Workers Union, protesters questioned the slaying of Emmett Till. A. Philip Randolph, organizer of the first African American labor union—the Brotherhood of Sleeping Car Porters—gave a powerful speech calling on people to fight against racism and social injustice.

The Montgomery Bus Boycott

Two months later, on December 1, 1955, Rosa Parks, a seamstress in Montgomery, Alabama, rode a city bus. The

Rosa Parks being fingerprinted by police.

driver ordered her to give up her seat to a white man. The soft-spoken but fearless woman refused. She was immediately arrested. She had violated the city's racial segregation law: blacks sitting in the back of public buses must give up their seats to white riders if the other front seats were full.

Parks was also the secretary of the local NAACP chapter. Word of her arrest rapidly spread. The city's black leaders quickly organized a one-day boycott of the city's buses. They knew that 70 percent of the bus riders in the city were black. On December 5, 90 percent of the black community did not ride the buses.[5] The boycott was a great success. It led to the formation of the Montgomery Improvement Association (MIA). Its purpose was to mobilize more protests.

The MIA appointed as their leader a 26-year-old preacher with a powerful voice named Martin Luther King Jr. He stood at the pulpit of the Holt Street Baptist Church on December 5, 1955. Thousands of people crowded inside and outside the building. King talked about the bravery of Rosa Parks and the upcoming boycott: "We are not here advocating violence. . . . The only weapon that we have in our hands this evening is the weapon of protest. . . . And we are determined

Martin Luther King on the first bus after the boycott's success.

here in Montgomery—to work and fight until justice runs down like water and righteousness like a mighty stream!"[6]

People clapped, stomped their feet, and roared their approval.

King finished his speech with this: "Let us go out with a grim and bold determination that we are going to stick together. . . . When the history books are written . . . somebody will have to say, there lived a race of people, black people . . . who had the moral courage to stand up for their rights."[7]

King was vital in leading the long Montgomery bus boycott. Many other activists joined him, including Bayard Rustin, Jo Ann Robinson, E.D. Nixon, and the Reverend Ralph David Abernathy. King and Abernathy were close associates. Like James Farmer, they had also studied Mahatma Gandhi's principles of nonviolence.

The bus boycott continued for over twelve months. Montgomery's black citizens were cooperative and supportive of each other. Churches organized private taxis and carpools to transport people to work. Thousands walked miles to work and back home, refusing to ride segregated buses.[8]

White resistance was fierce. King's and Nixon's homes and Abernathy's church were bombed. Carpool drivers were stopped and issued tickets for minor reasons. There were acts of violence, police harassment, and arrests. But the boycotts continued until the MIA was victorious. The U.S. Supreme Court ruled on November 13 that Alabama's bus segregation seating policy was unconstitutional.

The success achieved by MIA inspired bus boycotts across the country. It also thrust Martin Luther King Jr. into the national spotlight.[9]

MUSIC AND THE MOVEMENT

Music played a powerful role in the civil rights movement, including music as varied as black spirituals, gospel, folk, rhythm and blues, and jazz. People sang in churches, community meetings, marches, and even in jail. Martin Luther King Jr. called music "the soul of the movement." He said freedom songs "give people new courage and a sense of unity. I think they keep alive faith, a radiant hope in the future, particularly in our most trying hours."[10]

Men, women, and children performed these freedom songs. It was common during protests to hear songs like "Keep Your Eyes on the Prize," "We Shall Overcome," "Ain't You Got a Right to the Tree of Life," "Oh Freedom," "We Shall Not Be Moved," "This Little Light of Mine," and "Lift Every Voice and Sing."

While many songs were uplifting, some of them captured the tragic events of the era. Billie Holiday's "Strange Fruit" was about the horror of lynching. Jazz musician John Coltrane wrote the emotional instrumental "Alabama" after four black girls were killed in a church bombing in Birmingham. "People Get Ready" by Curtis Mayfield & The Impressions is filled with the promise and excitement of the civil rights movement. "A Change Is Gonna Come" by Sam Cooke dealt with the struggle and hope for world change.[11]

Sam Cooke

CHAPTER THREE
Sit-Ins and Freedom Rides

On February 1, 1960, in Greensboro, North Carolina, four black friends sat down at the segregated Woolworth's white lunch counter and ordered coffee and doughnuts. The men—Ezell Blair Jr. (now Jibreel Khazan), Franklin McCain, Joseph McNeil, and David Richmond—were freshmen from the all-black North Carolina Agricultural and Technical College. The waitresses ignored their requests. A police officer arrived on the scene and paced back and forth behind the freshmen. He slapped his billy club in his hand, not sure what to do. The store manager tried to convince the students to leave, but they politely refused. The peaceful young men sat unserved until the store closed. They told the staff they would be back.[1]

By the time the men returned to campus, everyone knew about their sit-in. Student leaders met with them and organized a follow-up protest. The next day, over a dozen more black students joined them at the lunch counter. The day after that, so many students, black and white, became a part of the sit-in it disrupted downtown business activities. By the end of the month, the mayor of Greensboro was working to negotiate the

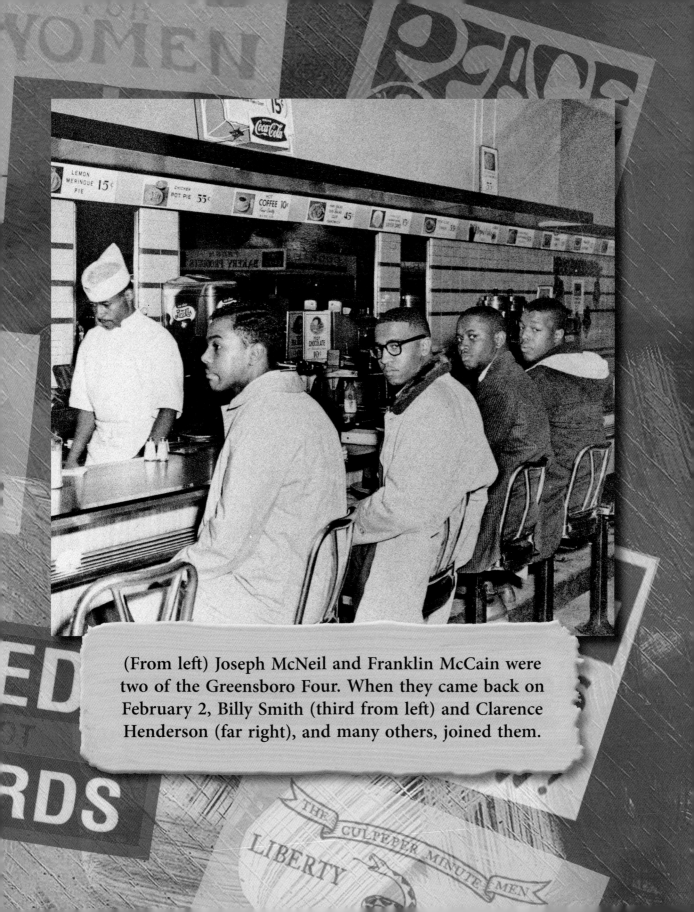

(From left) Joseph McNeil and Franklin McCain were two of the Greensboro Four. When they came back on February 2, Billy Smith (third from left) and Clarence Henderson (far right), and many others, joined them.

student's demands. Media coverage of the event triggered more nonviolent sit-ins throughout the South.

The rapid growth of sit-ins soon led to violent reactions. The white community saw the protesters as "agitators." People who wanted to participate in sit-ins received training on how to act in a nonviolent manner. Civil rights activist Reverend James Lawson held workshops in Nashville. As the sit-ins spread, angry whites attacked people, yanking them from their stools and punching and kicking them. They dumped condiments, drinks, and food on them. There were even reports of nonviolent protesters being burned with cigarettes. The police harassed protesters, beating them with clubs and throwing them in jail for disorderly conduct. The protesters kept their cool and did not retaliate.

By July, the Greensboro Woolworth's finally integrated the counter where it all started. The success of the sit-ins and these young protesters grew to be the main focus of the movement. Sit-ins were used to integrate parks, swimming pools, theaters, libraries, and other public facilities.

The Freedom Riders

In 1961, James Farmer, head of the Congress of Racial Equality (CORE), organized a follow-up to the Journey of Reconciliation. This time it was called the "Freedom Rides." Thirteen trained black and white volunteers, this time including both men and women, left Washington, D.C., on May 4, 1961, for the first Freedom Ride into the South. John Lewis of the Student Nonviolent Coordinating Committee (SNCC) and James Peck, a veteran of the 1947 Journey, joined them. Two groups set out on the second journey by interstate bus. The plan was to target facilities on the road, including waiting rooms, restrooms, and restaurants.[2]

The Freedom Riders met violent resistance along the way. They were first violently attacked on May 12 in Rock Hill, South Carolina, where they split between two interstate buses.

On Mother's Day, May 14, 1961, the Riders on one of the buses were attacked by a mob of around 200 white people in Anniston, Alabama. Their bus was firebombed, and as the Freedom Riders escaped, they were beaten by the surrounding mob.

When the Freedom Riders on the other bus reached Birmingham, another enraged white mob attacked them. Several riders were severely injured. The images of burning buses and injured riders appeared in newspapers around the country, drawing international attention; however, Alabama Governor John Patterson argued on television that he could not protect the riders. He called them "a bunch of rabble-rousers."[3]

James Farmer (holding briefcase) boards a Freedom Ride bus headed for the Deep South.

The violence didn't stop the Freedom Riders. Their commitment deepened and more sought to join their cause. In Nashville, civil rights activist Diane Nash met with Fred Shuttlesworth, a Birmingham minister and co founder of the Southern Christian Leadership Conference (SCLC). She told him that her students wanted to come to Birmingham and continue the Freedom Ride.

Shuttlesworth remarked, "Do you know that the Freedom Riders were almost killed here?"

Nash replied: "Yes, that's exactly why the ride must not be stopped. If they stop us with violence, the movement is dead. We're coming!"[4]

The Nashville students boarded a bus to Birmingham on May 17. They were attacked and harassed, as well, but they kept coming back. The Nashville riders also traveled to Montgomery, Alabama. Finally, Attorney General Robert F. Kennedy negotiated with Governor Patterson to arrange for a driver and protection for the

Diane Nash and her students singing outside the Nashville police station in 1961 to protest police brutality against lunch counter activists.

riders. The trip resumed with police escort on May 20. When the police abandoned the riders in Montgomery, Alabama, Kennedy called in federal marshals to guard them instead. The Freedom Riders continued their quest into the state of Mississippi.

That summer, over 300 Freedom Riders were arrested. While trying to work out a deal with the Mississippi senator, President John F. Kennedy and Attorney General Robert Kennedy asked the civil rights leaders for a "cooling-off" period. Farmer responded: "We have been cooling off now for the past 350 years. If we cool off anymore, we'll be in a deep freeze."[5]

The Freedom Riders achieved their goal. In September 1961, the U.S. Interstate Commerce Commission banned segregated facilities in bus and train stations nationwide.

The South had largely ignored the 1946 ruling that segregation in interstate travel was unconstitutional. Despite the courage of the black and white bus riders during the Journey of Reconciliation, the South maintained its Jim Crow laws. Bus travel remained segregated. Both the Montgomery Bus Boycott and the Freedom Riders were more successful. They had the strength and power of massive protests behind them.

THE REVEREND JAMES LAWSON AND HIS NONVIOLENT WORKSHOPS

Religious student James Lawson was 30 years old when he was jailed for opposing the Korean War. He got out on parole and was sent by his church to India as a missionary. In India, he learned about Mahatma Gandhi and how he used passive resistance to battle racial prejudice. When he returned to the United States, Lawson discussed Gandhi's nonviolent tactics with Martin Luther King Jr. in detail during the Montgomery Bus Boycott. Lawson began conducting workshops in nonviolence throughout the South.[6] He was teaching in Nashville when four black men launched the sit-in at the Woolworth's lunch counter in Greensboro, North Carolina.

Because of all the media attention, by the end of that first week, hundreds of students came to Lawson's workshop. They wanted to be trained to be part of the sit-in movement in Nashville. Martin Luther King Jr. referred to the Nashville sit-in movement as the largest and most organized of them all. In those very tough workshops, black and white students practiced nonviolent tactics. They learned how to behave when people called them terrible names, hit and knocked them down, blew cigarette smoke into their face, spit on them, or worse. The students had to respond with love and dignity. They were taught: "Don't strike back or curse if abused . . . show yourself courteous and friendly at all times. . . . Remember love and nonviolence."[7] Some of the most famous civil rights leaders were trained in these workshops.

James Lawson (left) with Martin Luther King Jr.

CHAPTER FOUR
Mass Protests and Marches

In 1963, there were many demonstrations. More than 930 demonstrations were held throughout the South. Scores of additional demonstrations were held in Northern and Western cities.[1] One of the best-known protests occurred in Alabama's largest city, Birmingham. It was also the most segregated city in America, with a frightening history of racial violence.

Martin Luther King Jr. and SCLC leader Fred Shuttlesworth planned a citywide protest. They wanted to wage war on Jim Crow laws and push for fair hiring. They also wanted to desegregate public places, including schools, lunch counters, bus terminals, elevators, and parks. Shuttlesworth remarked, "We wanted confrontation, nonviolent confrontation to see if it would work on a massive scale. Not for just Birmingham—for the nation."[2]

In early April 1963, thousands of protesters joined the campaign in Birmingham.[3] The city's hostile police commissioner, Eugene "Bull" Connor, again fiercely refused to obey the federal court orders. He did everything in his power to maintain segregation in Birmingham. He closed city parks,

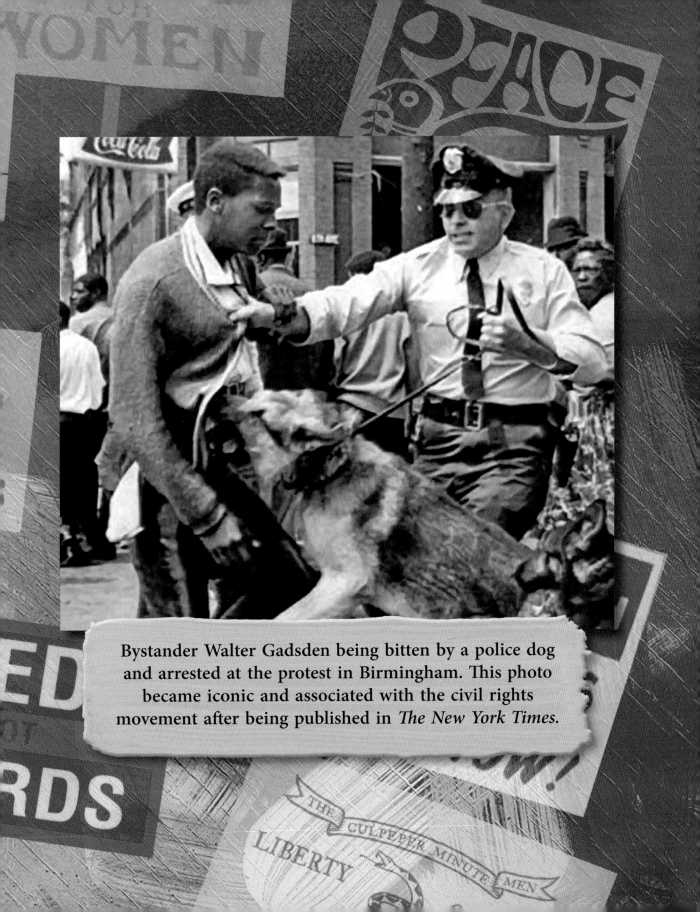

Bystander Walter Gadsden being bitten by a police dog and arrested at the protest in Birmingham. This photo became iconic and associated with the civil rights movement after being published in *The New York Times*.

swimming pools, playgrounds, and golf courses instead of agreeing to desegregate. The protesters knew the march in Birmingham could be very dangerous. The city had earned the name "Bombingham" because African American houses, churches, and businesses were targeted so often.[4]

King was arrested along with other protesters and thrown into solitary confinement. While there, he wrote "Letter from a Birmingham Jail," a powerful appeal for nonviolent civil disobedience.

The campaign continued, but many adults did not march. They were afraid of being arrested or losing their jobs. The young people carried the baton instead.

On Thursday, May 2, over 1,000 schoolchildren marched into the city's segregated Kelly Ingram Park. These young troopers were immediately taken to jail. But another "Children's Crusade" showed up and marched the next day. With the jails jam-packed with protesters, Bull Connor took another approach. He ordered the protesters to be sprayed with fire hoses. During their peaceful walk,

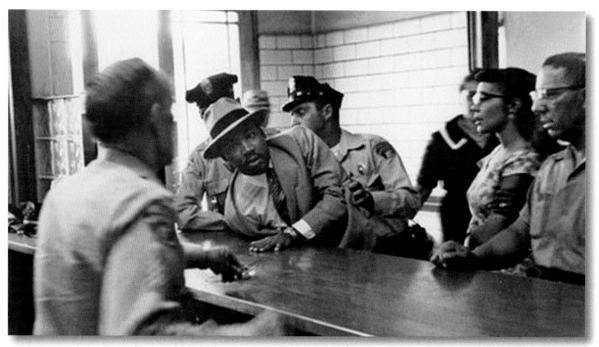

Dr. King arrested in Birmingham, Alabama.

Birmingham Commissioner of Public Safety Bull Connor ordered the use of fire hoses on protesters. In 1962, the city of Birmingham voted to replace the position of Commissioner of Public Safety. By June 1963, Bull Connor was out of a job.

black high school students were hit with high-pressure jets of water. They were beaten with clubs and attacked by police dogs. Many had to go to the hospital.[5]

The violent images were shown on TV. They exposed millions of Americans to the prejudice African Americans faced daily. Many of these viewers were witnessing this type of racism for the first time. They became sympathetic to the young people who were willing to go to jail for their beliefs.

The Kennedy administration finally made a stronger effort to reduce the crisis. Government officials pressured business leaders in the city to change their policies. As a peaceful resolution, the business leaders agreed to desegregate stores and hire more black workers.

Asa Philip Randolph championed labor rights for African Americans. He was the head of the 1963 March on Washington.

The March on Washington

During World War II, defense industries in the United States were growing quickly. Thousands of jobs were available. However, black men and women were not being hired for these jobs. Civil rights leaders agreed to plan a massive march in Washington, D.C. The president of the Brotherhood of Sleeping Car Porters, A. Philip Randolph, thought of the plan for the "March on Washington" movement. Randolph organized the march to pressure President Franklin D. Roosevelt to change these unfair labor practices.

The pressure worked. In 1941, the President issued an executive order banning discrimination in the defense industries and establishing the Fair Employment Practice Committee (FEPC) to investigate charges of racial discrimination. Randolph canceled the march.

Randolph's idea was still strong, and he lived to see his dream turn into reality. Civil rights activist Bayard Rustin organized a tremendous event on the National Mall in Washington, D.C. On August 28, 1963, over 200,000 people attended the March on Washington for Jobs and Freedom. In the sweltering afternoon heat, the audience was treated to speeches and music. The grand finale was reserved for Martin Luther King Jr. This was when he delivered his powerful "I Have a Dream" speech. It excited not just the crowd, but the entire country. King was a force that day. His words were both passionate and poetic. After this moving speech, King was hailed as the spokesman for black America.

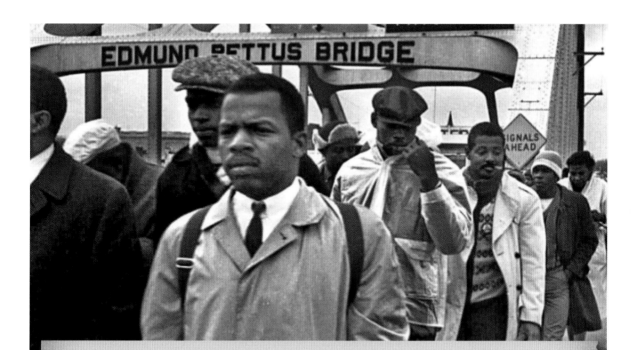

Future congressman and civil rights activist John Lewis (foreground). On March 7, 1965, Lewis led 600 peaceful marchers over the Edmund Pettus Bridge in Selma, Alabama.

The Selma to Montgomery March

In January 1965, the SCLC focused on registering black voters in Selma, Alabama. Governor George Wallace and Sheriff Jim Clark were openly against allowing blacks to vote. Clark proudly wore a badge that stated, "NEVER!" As a result, only 2 percent of Selma's eligible black voters had been registered. At a February 18 protest, Jimmie Lee Jackson, a peaceful protester, was killed.

The SCLC announced a massive protest march, motivated at least in part by outrage at Jackson's death. It would cover 54 miles, from Selma to Montgomery, the state capital. On Sunday, March 7, 600 marchers crossed the Edmund Pettus Bridge outside of Selma. Armed troopers attacked them. The troopers, on foot and riding horses, used whips, nightsticks, and tear gas. Dozens of people were injured, including John Lewis, whose skull was fractured. The brutal scene was called "Bloody Sunday."[6]

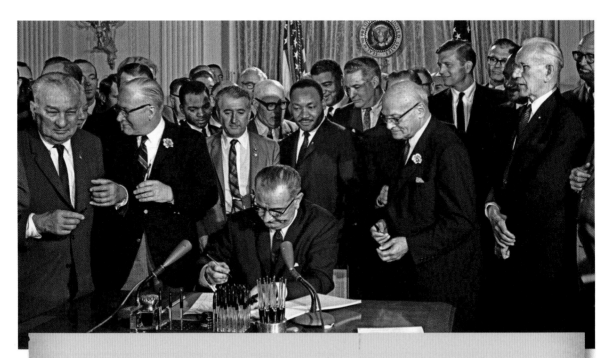

President Lyndon B. Johnson signs the Voting Rights Act into law, guaranteeing African Americans the right to vote. King and other civil rights leaders stand behind him.

Martin Luther King Jr. led more than 2,000 marchers on March 9, but they turned around when blocked by state troopers. The U.S. District Court stepped in and ordered Alabama to permit the march. On March 21, King led over 2,000 people on the three-day journey. This time, they were protected by the U.S. Army and the Alabama National Guard.

President Lyndon B. Johnson showed support for the Selma protesters and called for the passage of a new voting rights bill. He signed the Voting Rights Act into law on August 6, 1965. States were no longer allowed to prevent black people from registering to vote.

Johnson also signed the Fair Housing Act of 1968. This act prohibited discrimination in the sale, rental, and financing of homes. The President signed it on April 11, one week after Martin Luther King Jr. was assassinated in Memphis.

THE BAY AREA MARCH AGAINST JOB DISCRIMINATION

In 1960, African American organizations in Berkeley, San Francisco, and Oakland, California, met to form a new group. They created the Ad Hoc Committee To End Racial Discrimination. One of its goals was to end racism in job hiring. Their plan was to pressure businesses to hire more minority employees. White business owners claimed that black workers would scare away their white customers.[7]

In 1963, the Committee organized nonviolent marches and sit-ins throughout the Bay Area. Hundreds of these protesters were arrested.[8] The Committee picketed Mel's Drive-In, San Francisco's Sheraton-Palace Hotel, automobile dealerships, Lucky's grocery stores, and other businesses. They also picketed Oakland's Tribune Tower, the home of the *Oakland Tribune* newspaper. Although a few people were hired, overall, the Committee's demands were not met. Businesses failed to hire more black workers. In 1967, unemployment was still very high among blacks, especially those under age 25.[9]

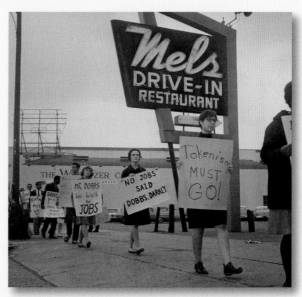

In 1963, student members of the Ad Hoc Committee to End Racial Discrimination picketed Mel's Drive-In.

CHAPTER FIVE
Modern Civil Rights Protests

This is a Movement, Not a Moment!
—*Chant heard at Black Lives Matter protest march
in Washington, D.C. (2016)*

Even after the civil rights laws were passed in the 1960s,
discrimination continued. Meanwhile, Martin Luther King Jr.'s
vision of a society where all people have equal rights thrived.
It greatly influenced the ongoing civil rights movement. And it
prompted people in the United States to protest discrimination in
other countries as well as at home.

The Tupelo March and Boycott

In 1976, in the small city of Tupelo, Mississippi, two white police
officers severely beat a black man. The man, Eugene Pasto, filed
a lawsuit against them, and a federal court ruled in his favor.
Outraged by the brutality, black citizens wanted the officers
to be fired. White council members disagreed. Instead, they
offered to transfer the officers to another department. The black
community saw this move as an insult. Several years before,

In 1978, poultry factory workers went on strike
and marched with the United League.

Skip Robinson

Alfred "Skip" Robinson had formed a grassroots movement named the United League. Its goal was to address school integration, job discrimination, and other issues relating to the rights of African Americans.[1] The United League stepped in to help the people of Tupelo.

In March, 1978, more than 400 people demonstrated against the police brutality. The black community also boycotted white-owned businesses in downtown Tupelo. The demonstrators demanded that more black people be hired across the city. Robinson called for a second march in June.

The Ku Klux Klan (KKK) planned a countermarch on the same day. The National Guard stationed 65 riot gear–clad police along the planned march route. However, conflict was avoided. The United League marchers changed the start time of their march to avoid confrontation with the KKK marchers. The United League boycotts remained until the city employed more black workers.[2]

The Free South Africa Movement

On Thanksgiving eve in 1984, four well-known black activists walked into the South African Embassy on Massachusetts Avenue in Washington, D.C. The four had a meeting with the South African Ambassador to ask for the release of political prisoners, such as Nelson Mandela, and to highlight human rights abuses in South Africa. When the ambassador refused, they conducted a sit-in. They demanded an end to apartheid, a brutal system of racial injustice in South Africa. The country had 23 million black citizens and 4.5 million whites. The government, run by whites, oppressed the black citizens in many ways. The races had limited contact. All places, including whole neighborhoods, were separated according to race. Mixed-race families were torn apart. And black people were not allowed to vote. Nelson Mandela led a freedom movement there, but he was arrested. By 1984, he had been a political prisoner for 20 years.[3]

Three of the embassy protesters were handcuffed to police cars and then jailed. They were Randall Robinson, founder and executive director of the policy group TransAfrica; Mary Frances Berry, U.S. Civil Rights Commissioner; and D.C. Congressman Walter E. Fauntroy. Eleanor Holmes Norton, Georgetown University law professor, had left before the arrests to address the media outside the embassy.

The embassy arrests became international news, and the Free South Africa Movement (FSAM) was born in the United States. Daily protests began outside the embassy and in South African consulates around the county. Within the next couple of years, thousands of demonstrators were arrested.

There was a huge number of grassroots actions in churches, on campuses, and among the unions. Coretta Scott King and Rosa Parks joined the demonstrations as the crowds sang, "We Shall Overcome."[4] The intense public pressure forced President Ronald Reagan to publicly condemn apartheid.

Coretta Scott King joined the protests against apartheid in South Africa. She and others were arrested for demonstrating within 500 feet of the South African Embassy.

During this period, protesters, who were called "messengers," chanted, "Free Nelson Mandela!" Celebrities such as tennis star Arthur Ashe and musician Stevie Wonder flew in to join the protests. They were also arrested. College students pressured their boards of trustees to sell the stock they owned in companies doing business with the South African government.

In 1986, the U.S. Congress passed the Comprehensive Anti-Apartheid Act, and sanctions were placed on South Africa. In 1990, hundreds of U.S. companies stopped doing business with South Africa. It cost South Africa at least a billion dollars. Finally, Nelson Mandela was released from prison. In 1994, South Africa adopted a new constitution. It gave blacks the right to vote and called for the election of a president. They voted for Nelson Mandela.[5]

In 1993, Nelson Mandela (right) and South African President F.W. de Klerk were given the Nobel Peace Prize. A year later, Mr. Mandela replaced him as president.

Children grab signs to join in the Afton protest to stop dump trucks from hauling toxic soil into the area in 1982.

The Afton "Lie-Down" Protest

In 1982, 10 yellow dump trucks drove to a new landfill site at Afton, in rural Warren County, North Carolina. The trucks carried six tons of soil contaminated with cancer-inducing toxins. At the site stood 60 riot gear–equipped patrol officers ready to confront over 100 black protesters. The marchers lay down on the road in front of the approaching trucks. The trucks stopped, but the officers arrested 55 demonstrators to clear the road. The trucks then dropped their toxic loads.

The Afton "lie-down" developed into a national movement. The next morning, more protesters arrived and laid down on the road. Local activists and civil rights leaders around the country flew in. Hundreds of demonstrators were arrested, and the lie-down protests made the national news.

The local pastor, Luther Brown said: "We know why they picked us. . . . Because it's a poor county and mostly black. . . . Nobody thought people like us would make a fuss."[6]

The protesters could not stop the landfills. Trucks dumped tens of thousands of cubic yards of toxic soil. Still, the story received a huge amount of publicity.

Because of Afton, in 1991, black activists widened their focus to include environmental racism. Over 1,000 activists met for the First National People of Color Environmental Leadership Summit. Demonstrations put pressure on the federal government. Veteran civil rights activist John Lewis and Senator Al Gore introduced an environmental bill to Congress. When Gore became vice president, President Bill Clinton signed an executive order. The order directed federal agencies to identify and address any bad environmental effects their programs would have on people of color.[7]

The Million Man March

On October 16, 1995, an estimated 870,000 African American men attended the "Million Man March." The March was held at the National Mall in Washington, D.C. It called for black men to unify and address the ills of the black community. The goal was for black men to take responsibility for their lives, their families, and their communities, and to build a base of black political power. The march inspired over 1.5 million black men to register to vote.[8]

Many religious groups, businesses, schools, and community organizations participated in the march. Speakers and entertainers included the Reverend Jesse Jackson, Rosa Parks, Dick Gregory, Stevie Wonder, and Maya Angelou.

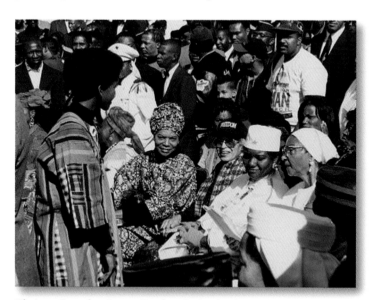

Elaine Steele, Rosa Parks, Ayinde Jean-Baptiste, and others join the Million Man March in Washington, D.C.

The Million Woman March

In 1997, the Million Woman March took place on October 25. It is estimated that 750,000 African American women from across the country gathered to march on the Ben Franklin Parkway in Philadelphia. The march started at the Liberty Bell and ended on the steps of the Philadelphia Museum of Art. Grassroots activists Phile Chionesu and Asia Coney organized the march. Its mission was to bring women together to discuss such issues as strengthening black families, finding a common voice in politics and civil rights, and battling the negative images of black women in popular culture and the media.[9]

The goal of the Million Woman March in 1997 was to rebuild black communities. An estimated 750,000 women gathered to march on the Ben Franklin Parkway in Philadelphia.

Black Lives Matter Protests

During the summer of 2013, three community organizers—Alicia Garza, Patrisse Cullors, and Ayọ Tometi—founded the Black Lives Matter (BLM) movement. They shared a passion for fighting social injustice, and they found each other on social media after the murder of Trayvon Martin. Martin was an unarmed 17-year-old who was killed by George Zimmerman, a neighborhood watch coordinator. Zimmerman was later acquitted of the killing. The verdict produced tremendous outrage in the black community.

The women understood the history of the nonviolent struggle of the civil rights movement, and they recognized the power of social media to mobilize the community. On August 9, 2014, 18-year-old Michael Brown was killed by police officer Darren Wilson. This time, BLM was ready. Hundreds of BLM

In 2016, Black Lives Matter shut down city streets in downtown Baltimore with peaceful rallies, marches, and sit-ins.

members from cities throughout the nation gathered to protest and demonstrate against the police shooting. Protesters chanted, "Hands up! Don't shoot!" News stories about these events pushed the issue of police brutality onto the national and international stage.[10]

Between 2014 and 2015, Black Lives Matter chapters had organized more than 950 protest demonstrations against police actions involving the deaths of black citizens.[11] Their demonstrations have prompted investigations into police misconduct across the country. In 2014, the U.S. Congress enacted the Death in Custody Reporting Act. The Act requires states to document and report all deaths at the hands of police that occur during an arrest.

Black Lives Matter protests have continued around the country. In 2016, Alton Sterling was shot by police in Baton Rouge, Louisiana. Hundreds of people gathered to protest, and 100 were arrested. Among them was Ieshia Evans, a nurse and mother, who stood stock still while police in riot gear

Ieshia Evans stands calmly as riot police advance during a Black Lives Matter protest.

handcuffed her. She later wrote, "I wasn't afraid. I took a stand in Baton Rouge because enough is enough."[12]

MORE HEROINES OF CIVIL RIGHTS

Dorothy Height

President Barack Obama called Dorothy Height "the godmother of the Civil Rights Movement."[13] In 1946, Height helped to direct the integration of all the YWCA Centers. She was president of the National Council for Negro Women for 40 years. She formed the Center for Racial Justice in 1965. She helped to organize the March on Washington. She also organized workshops to help freedom schools and provided help to poor families.

Fannie Lou Hamer

Fannie Lou Hamer came from a large family of Mississippi sharecroppers. In 1962, she became a civil rights activist. She championed registering black people to vote in Mississippi. For her courageous efforts she was threatened, shot at, arrested, and beaten so badly she had kidney damage, a limp, and lost vision in one of her eyes for the rest of her life. She helped establish the Mississippi Freedom Democratic Party. Besides her devotion to helping families in need, she is remembered for her dynamic and fiery speech at the Democratic National Convention in 1964. She spoke about the resistance and violence she and other blacks experienced in Mississippi while they were trying to register voters. By the time she finished, she had become the heart of the convention.

1863	President Abraham Lincoln signs the Emancipation Proclamation, which frees the slaves in the United States.
1868	The Fourteenth Amendment is ratified: African Americans may not be denied equal protection or due process of law.
1870	The Fifteenth Amendment is ratified, giving black men the right to vote.
1875	Civil Rights Act of 1875 prohibits racial discrimination and guarantees equal access to public accommodations.
1877	Reconstruction ends in the South. Civil rights for blacks are no longer protected.
1896	*Plessy v. Ferguson* holds that racial segregation is constitutional. It opens the door for Jim Crow laws in the South.
1909	The National Association for the Advancement of Colored People is founded. Its publication *The Crisis* is launched, with the first issue releasing in 1910.
1914	Marcus Garvey establishes the Universal Negro Improvement Association "to promote the spirit of race pride."
1941	President Theodore Roosevelt signs an executive order that bans discrimination against minorities in defense contracts.
1948	President Harry S. Truman issues an executive order integrating the U.S. Armed Forces.
1954	In *Brown v. Board of Education of Topeka*, the U.S. Supreme Court rules that racial segregation in schools is unconstitutional.
1955	Emmett Till is murdered. Rosa Parks refuses to give up her seat at the front of the "colored section" of a bus in Montgomery, Alabama, to a white passenger, defying a Southern law. It leads to a successful year-long bus boycott led by Martin Luther King Jr.
1957	The Southern Christian Leaders Conference is established. Federal troops are sent to protect nine African-American students (now known as the Little Rock Nine) from white mobs trying to block integration at Central High School in Little Rock, Arkansas.
1960	Four black students in Greensboro, North Carolina, begin a sit-in at a segregated Woolworth's lunch counter. The event triggers nonviolent protests throughout the South. The Student Nonviolent Coordinating Committee is founded, providing young blacks a place in the civil rights movement.
1961	Congress of Racial Equality (CORE) organizes the Freedom Rides into the South to test new laws prohibiting segregation in interstate travel facilities. Bus riders are attacked by angry mobs.
1963	Martin Luther King writes "Letter from Birmingham Jail." At the March on Washington for Jobs and Freedom, King delivers his famous "I Have a Dream" speech. Four black girls are killed when a bomb explodes at a church in Birmingham. Mississippi Freedom Summer voter education and registration project begins. Two white and one black student volunteers are murdered. President John F. Kennedy is assassinated.
1964	President Lyndon B. Johnson signs the Civil Rights Act. Martin Luther King Jr. receives the Nobel Peace Prize.
1965	The Voting Rights Act is signed into law. Black nationalist Malcolm X is assassinated. The Watts section of Los Angeles explodes into six days of rioting. On Bloody Sunday, troops attack the Selma to Montgomery marchers. Another larger march is successful.

Year	Event
1966	The Black Panthers are founded by Huey Newton and Bobby Seale. Stokely Carmichael, head of the SNCC, coins the term "Black Power" during a voter registration drive in Mississippi.
1967	President Johnson appoints African American Thurgood Marshall to the Supreme Court. The Supreme Court rules in *Loving v. Virginia* that prohibiting interracial marriage is unconstitutional.
1968	Martin Luther King Jr. is assassinated in Memphis. The Civil Rights Act of 1968 is signed by President Johnson. Shirley Chisholm becomes the first black female U.S. Representative.
1971	The Supreme Court in *Swann v. Charlotte-Mecklenburg Board of Education* upholds busing as a legitimate means for achieving integration of public schools.
1972	Shirley Chisholm is the first African American woman to run for president.
1987	Congress passes the Civil Rights Restoration Act, overriding President Ronald Reagan's veto. It expands nondiscrimination laws within private institutions that receive federal funds.
1992	Race riots erupt after a Los Angeles jury acquits four white police officers of the beating of Rodney King.
1994	After worldwide protests against apartheid, South Africa adopts a new constitution and elects Nelson Mandela as president.
2001	Colin Powell becomes the first African American U.S. Secretary of State.
2005	Condoleezza Rice becomes the first black female U.S. Secretary of State.
2008	Barack Obama is the first African American to be elected president of the United States.
2013	After the man who killed Trayvon Martin is acquitted, Alicia Garza, Patrisse Cullors, and Ayọ Tometi form Black Lives Matter.
2014	The killing of unarmed 18-year-old Michael Brown by officer Darren Wilson sparks protests in Ferguson, Missouri, and cities across the United States. Congress enacts the Death in Custody Reporting Act.
2016	San Francisco 49ers quarterback Colin Kaepernick takes a knee during the national anthem to protest police brutality and oppression of people of color. It gains international attention.
2017	In January nearly 2,000 mostly black protesters march near Washington's Martin Luther King Jr. Memorial for minority rights and to preserve the Affordable Care Act.
2020	The murder of jogger Ahmaud Arbery by a white father and son in Georgia, the killing of Breonna Taylor during a botched no-knock police raid, and the murder of George Floyd all occurred within a three-month span, kicking off global demonstrations in support of the Black Lives Matter movement. Many federal and state policing laws were changed as a result.
2021	Vice President Kamala Harris is sworn in. She is the first woman vice president as well as the first Black and South Asian American vice president.

Chapter 1: Civil Rights Protests—The Beginnings

1. "Confrontational Abolitionism," *The Abolition Seminar.* https://www.abolitionseminar.org/confrontational-abolitionism/

2. "Cival Rights Leaders" https://naacp.org/find-resources/history-explained/civil-rights-leaders

3. Patricia Sullivan. *Lift Every Voice: The NAACP and the Making of the Civil Rights Movement* (New York: The New Press, 2009), pp. 48–49.

4. Dick Lehr, "When 'Birth of a Nation' Sparked a Riot in Boston," *Boston Globe*, October 5, 2016, https://www.bostonglobe.com/ideas/2016/10/05/when-birth-nation-sparked-riot-boston/bN9S0ltko6QyRIQiJcr9KJ/story.html

5. Sullivan, pp. 68–69.

6. "The First Massive African American Protest in U.S. History Was Led by Children Marching Against Lynching in the Silent Protest Parade," *Black Then*, November 11, 2016, https://blackthen.com/first-massive-african-american-protest-in-u-s-history-was-led-by-children-marching-against-lynching-in-the-silent-protest-parade/

7. James Farmer, *Lay Bare the Heart: An Autobiography of the Civil Rights Movement* (Fort Worth: Texas Christian University Press, 1985), pp. 106–107.

8. George Hauser, "The Freedom Rides: From Project to Mass Movement." Fellowship of Reconciliation USA Archives.

9. CORE: "George Houser (1927–) Co-Founder, Congress of Racial Equality," https://www.thecongressofracialequality.org/george-houser.html

10. "Mahatma Gandhi," Biography, https://www.biography.com/political-figures/mahatma-gandhi

11. Ibid.

12. "Non-violence," BBC Ethics Guide, 2014, https://www.bbc.co.uk/ethics/war/against/nonviolence.shtml

Chapter 2: Civil Rights Activities in the 1950s

1. "May 1952: RCNL Holds First Mass Meeting in Mississippi Delta." Digital SNCC Gateway. https://snccdigital.org/events/rcnl-holds-first-mass-meeting-mississippi-delta/

2. "Regional Council of Negro Leadership Established in Mississippi." Veterans of the Civil Rights Movement—History and Timeline, 1951–1953. https://www.crmvet.org/tim/timhis51.htm

3. Steven Kasher, *The Civil Rights Movement: A Photographic History, 1954–68* (New York: Abbeville Press Publishers, 2000), p. 11.

4. Yvonne Ryan, *Roy Wilkins: The Quiet Revolutionary and the NAACP* (Lexington: The University Press of Kentucky, 2014), p. 55.

5. Ryan, pp. 55–56.

6. Taylor Branch, *The King Years: Historic Moments in the Civil Rights Movement* (New York, Simon & Schuster, 2013), pp. 8–11.

7. Kasher, p. 35.

8. James Farmer, *Lay Bare the Heart: An Autobiography of the Civil Rights Movement* (Fort Worth: Texas Christian University Press, 1985), p. 185.

9. Martin Luther King, Jr. *The Autobiography of Martin Luther King, Jr.* Edited by Clayborne Carson (New York: Hachette Book Group, 1998), n.p.

10. "Hope for America: Performers, Politics and Pop Culture Political Songs," Library of Congress, https://www.loc.gov/exhibits/hope-for-america/political-songs.html

11. "Top 10 Civil Rights Protest Songs of all Time," NEWSONE, n.d., https://newsone.com/1460645/top-10-civil-rights-protest-songs-of-all-time/

Chapter 3: Sit-Ins and Freedom Rides

1. Steven Kasher, *The Civil Rights Movement: A Photographic History, 1954–68* (New York: Abbeville Press Publishers, 2000), pp. 66-68.

2. James Farmer, *Lay Bare the Heart: An Autobiography of the Civil Rights Movement* (Fort Worth: Texas Christian University Press, 1985), pp. 196–197.

3. Kasher, pp. 75–76.
4. Ibid.
5. Ibid.
6. Kasher, p. 69.
7. "Jim Lawson Conducts Nonviolence Workshops in Nashville," SNCC Digital Gateway, https://snccdigital.org/events/ jim-lawson-conducts-nonviolent-workshops -in-nashville/

Chapter 4: Mass Protests and Marches

1. Stephen Tuck, *We Ain't What We Ought to Be: The Black Freedom Struggle From Emancipation to Obama* (Cambridge: Belknap Press, 2010), p. 295.
2. Steven Kasher, *The Civil Rights Movement: A Photographic History, 1954–68* (New York: Abbeville Press Publishers, 2000), p. 88.
3. Yvonne Ryan, *Roy Wilkins: The Quiet Revolutionary and the NAACP* (Lexington: The University Press of Kentucky, 2014), p. 108.
4. Kasher, p. 88.
5. Tuck, pp. 293–294.
6. Ryan, pp. 146–147.
7. "Civil Rights Marches Against Hiring Practices," Picture This, http://picturethis. museumca.org/timeline/unforgettable-change- 1960s/civil-rights/info
8. Carl Nolte, "S.F. Palace Hotel Sit-in Helped Start Revolution 50 years ago," *SFGate*, March 1, 2014, http://www.sfgate.com/bayarea/ article/S-F-Palace-Hotel-sit-in-helped-start- revolution-5279160.php
9. "Civil Rights Marches Against Hiring Practices," Picture This, http://picturethis. museumca.org/timeline/unforgettable-change- 1960s/civil-rights/info

Chapter 5: Modern Civil Rights Protests

1. Stephen Tuck, *We Ain't What We Ought to Be: The Black Freedom Struggle from Emancipation to Obama* (Cambridge: Belknap Press, 2010), p. 369.
2. "KKK/United League March," Mississippi Civil Rights Project.

3. Krissah Thompson, "On Mandela Day, D.C. Founders of Free South Africa Movement Look Back." *The Washington Post*, July 17, 2013. https://www.washingtonpost.com/ lifestyle/style/on-mandela-day-dc-founders-of- free-south-africa-movement-look- back/2013/07/17/61db5a5e-eee1-11e2-a1f9- ea873b7e0424_story.html
4. Tuck, pp. 379–380.
5. Thompson.
6. Tuck, pp. 383–384.
7. Ibid., p. 385.
8. "Million Man March, 1995," Blackpast.org. https://www.blackpast.org/african-american- history/events-african-american-history/ million-man-march-1995/
9. "Million Woman March, 1997." BlackPast.org Blog. https://www.blackpast.org/african- american-history/million-woman-march-1997/
10. "Black Lives Matter: The Growth of a New Social Justice Movement." https://www. blackpast.org/african-american-history/ black-lives-matter-growth-new-social-justice- movement/
11. Ibid.
12. Ieshia Evans, "I Wasn't Afraid. I Took a Stand in Baton Rouge Because Enough Is Enough." *The Guardian*, July 22, 2016, https://www. theguardian.com/commentisfree/2016/ jul/22/i-wasnt-afraid-i-took-a-stand-in-baton- rouge-because-enough-is-enough
13. Jesse Lee, "The Godmother of the Civil Rights Movement." White House Press Release, April 20, 2010, https://obamawhitehouse.archives. gov/blog/2010/04/20/godmother- civil-rights-movement

Works Consulted

Branch, Taylor. *The King Years: Historic Moments in the Civil Rights Movement.* New York: Simon & Schuster, 2013.

Farmer, James. *Lay Bare the Heart: An Autobiography of the Civil Rights Movement.* Fort Worth: Texas Christian University Press. 1986.

Friedman, Monroe. *Consumer Boycotts: Effecting Change Through the Marketplace and Media.* New York: Routledge, 1999.

Kasher, Steven. *The Civil Rights Movement: A Photographic History, 1954–68.* New York: Abbeville Press Publishers. 1996.

King, Martin Luther, Jr. *The Autobiography of Martin Luther King, Jr.* Edited by Clayborne Carson. New York: Hachette Book Group, 1998.

Ryan, Yvonne. *Roy Wilkins: The Quiet Revolutionary And The NAACP.* Lexington: University Press of Kentucky. 2014.

Sullivan, Patricia. *Lift Every Voice: The NAACP and the Making of the Civil Rights Movement.* New York: The New Press, 2009.

Tuck, Stephen. *We Ain't What We Ought to Be: The Black Freedom Struggle from Emancipation to Obama.* Cambridge: The Belknap Press, 2010.

Books

Adamson, Heather. *The Civil Rights Movement: An Interactive History Adventure (You Choose: History).* North Mankato, MN: Capstone Press, 2016.

Feldstein, Ruth. *How It Feels to Be Free: Black Women Entertainers and the Civil Rights Movement.* New York: Oxford University Press, 2013.

Lewis, John. *March: Book Three.* Marietta: Top Shelf Productions, 2016.

Shelton, Paula Young. *Child of the Civil Rights Movement.* Decorah, IA: Dragonfly Books. 2013.

Weatherford, Carole Boston. *Voice of Freedom: Fannie Lou Hamer: The Spirit of the Civil Rights Movement.* Somerville, MA: Candlewick Press, 2015.

Internet Reading

African-American Civil Rights Movement. Ducksters—Civil Rights.
https://www.ducksters.com/history/civil_rights/african-american_civil_rights_movement.php

Civil Rights Movement. John F. Kennedy Presidential Library And Museum.
https://www.jfklibrary.org/learn/about-jfk/jfk-in-history/civil-rights-movement

"The Legacy of the Civil Rights Movement." Virginia Museum of History & Culture. https://virginiahistory.org/learn/civil-rights-movement-virginia/legacy-civil-rights-movement

"March On Washington." History for Kids.
https://www.historyforkids.net/march-on-washington.html

"The Selma Marches for Voting Freedom." Social Studies for Kids.
https://socialstudiesforkids.com/articles/ushistory/selma-montgomerymarches.htm

GLOSSARY

abolitionist (ab-uh-LIH-shuh-nist)—A person who wants to end slavery.

acquit (uh-KWIT)—To declare that a person is not guilty of a crime.

agitator (AD-jih-tay-ter)—Someone who stirs unrest or controversy.

boycott (BOY-kot)—To refuse to buy, use, or participate in something as a way of protesting.

censor (SEN-ser)—To review books, movies, or other forms of communication to remove things that might be objectionable or harmful to society.

disobedience (dis-oh-BEE-dee-uns)—Refusal to obey laws or rules.

grassroots—Starting with the ordinary people in a society or organization.

interstate (IN-ter-stayt)—Involving more than one state.

Jim Crow laws—Laws that discriminated against blacks in the United States from approximately 1865–1968; unfair treatment of blacks through segregation.

mobilize (MOH-bul-yz)—To bring people together for an important action.

petition (peh-TIH-shun)—A formal written request made to a person in authority or organization.

reconciliation (reh-kun-sil-ee-AY-shun)—The act of bringing people or groups back together as friends after a disagreement.

resolution (reh-zuh-LOO-shun)—An answer or solution to a conflict or problem.

retaliate (ree-TAL-ee-ayt)—To do something bad to someone who has hurt you; to seek revenge.

sanctions (SANK-shuns)—Formal punishments, such as refusing to trade, used against a government in order to enforce a law.

segregate (SEH-greh-gayt)—To separate people because of their race or religion.

solidarity (sah-luh-DAYR-ih-tee)—A feeling of unity between people who have the same interests and goals.

stereotype (STAYR-ee-oh-typ)—An often unfair and untrue belief that people have about a particular group of people.

PHOTO CREDITS: Pp. 5, 9, 38—Loc.gov; p. 13—FBI.gov; p. 16—Everett Collection; p.25—NPS.gov; pp. 33, 34—fortunateson.us; p. 40—John Lucia, ThankHerForSurviving. All other photos—Public Domain. Every measure has been taken to find all copyright holders of material used in this book. In the event any mistakes or omissions have happened within, attempts to correct them will be made in future editions of the book.

WOMEN

PEACE
NOW

WE
MARCH
FOR
JOBS
FOR ALL
NOW!

EDS

RDS

THE
CULPEPER MINUTE MEN
LIBERTY